The Fun Book for Moms

Also by Melina Gerosa Bellows

Wish: A Novel
The Fun Book for Couples
The Fun Book

The Fun Book for Moms

102 Ways to Celebrate Family

Melina Gerosa Bellows

**Andrews McMeel
Publishing, LLC**

Kansas City

Attention: Schools and Businesses

Andrews McMeel books are available at quantity discounts with bulk purchase for
educational, business, or sales promotional use. For information, please write to:
Special Sales Department, Andrews McMeel Publishing, LLC,
4520 Main Street, Kansas City, Missouri 64111.

For Chase and Mackenzie

The most important thing she'd learned
over the years was that there was
no way to be a perfect mother
and a million ways to be a good one.

※ Jill Churchill, *Grime and Punishment*

Acknowledgments

As I am ridiculously blessed in the friend department, there are too many pals to name here. But a few I must. Heartfelt gratitude to Karen Hamilton, Lindsey Truitt, Isobel Coleman, Annie Belt, and Rebecca Ascher Walsh for whispering me through the dark woods and into the light. Special thanks to editrixes Barbara Graham and Susan O'Keefe, to idea geniuses Margaret Zackowitz, Kristin Starr, Mary Fehrnstrom, and Laura Quill, and to my willing researcher, Erin Bauer. Of course, *The Fun Book for Moms* wouldn't exist without the talents of my patient agent, Claudia Cross; gifted editor, Kelly Gilbert; and stylish illustrator Sarah Wilkins. I am grateful to my own mother for setting and tirelessly continuing to set such a stellar example. And most of all thank you to Keith for blessing me with my meerkats, Chase and Mackenzie, and being my hero in general.

Introduction

Nudie Scarf Dancing. That sounds provocative, sexy, or even NC-17, right? Well . . . not exactly. Let me explain.

I was sitting on the beach with my friend Isobel. Now, lounging next to this skinny blond mother of five could make anyone feel depressed by comparison. But I've known her since high school, I needed advice, and I figured she just might have some good insider tips. After all, in college Isobel was best buds with Brooke Shields, who admitted in her memoir that she knew a thing or two about the state I was in: Planet Ugly, aka postpartum depression.

I couldn't stop crying, and I alternated between being barely able to cope with the daily responsibilities of motherhood, and mind-numbing confusion. I was stumped. What did I have to be sad about? Seventeen months after giving birth to my son, Chase, God had blessed me with my daughter, Mackenzie. Instant family, my dream come true. Still, I felt as if I were sinking, drowning, and disappearing into toxic black ink.

My dirty secret was this: I just didn't see what was so great about motherhood. My days seemed like a marathon disaster movie starring me racing around after my kamikaze toddler to prevent him from hurling himself from high places, swallowing metal objects, and/or gleefully electrocuting himself. My nights were a protracted exercise in sleep deprivation, with Mackenzie getting up every two hours and screaming from acid reflux. Plus, talk about psychological whiplash. I had just experienced nine months of being treated like a pregnant princess, and now I felt as invisible as a ghost. A fat ghost.

I told Isobel about my plight, and she immediately flew into action, rattling off all of the wonderful ways she whiles away the hours with her brood: family *karaoke*, eating chocolate-chip-cookie batter together, firefly-catching contests. I was years away from all of this, but I scribbled the ideas down anyway. Then she mentioned Nudie Scarf Dancing.

"What's that?" I asked.

"Isn't it self-explanatory?" my skinny blond friend said.

I glanced down at my stretched-out stomach, which was lying next to me like an affectionate pet. Surely, she couldn't be suggesting . . .

The tears welled up in my eyes. I felt horrified and hopeless. There was just no way I was up for this, no matter how *fun* it was.

"Not *you*, silly!" she said, laughing so hard that she was beginning to snort. "*Daughters!* Don't you have a box of ugly silk scarves from the eighties that you have no clue what to do with? Turn on the music and it's a way to kill time with little girls before their baths!"

Isobel was now giggling so hard that she was on the verge of actually wetting herself. Before I knew it, I started laughing, too—at Isobel's snorting, at myself, and at the thought of the now-undulating pet attached to my midsection with a paisley scarf wrapped around it. Or maybe a feather *boa*. I laughed harder and harder until I was crying, too, a condition that Dolly Parton called her favorite emotion.

Then it hit me: *Fun* was going to show me the way out of my drowning pit! The relief of reclaiming my long-lost sense of humor embraced me like a bear hug. The problem wasn't that I was exhausted, scared, or despairing, because motherhood comes with all of that. The issue was that I wasn't having any fun to offset the exorbitant emotional cost.

I'm no stranger to the powerful, provocative, and even healing power of fun. Fun had first come to my rescue when I was single. My Knight in Shining Armor, fun never let me down even when my dates did. Back then, fun was a single girl's best friend. Possible anytime, anywhere, even when you least expected it, fun was a Zen master when it came to reducing stress, a zippy short-cut to living in the moment and a stealth bomber to life's cruelest indignities. Just when I was getting the hang of things—riding around in ragtops with my girlfriends, perfecting the dirty martini, and amusing myself by using my ex-boyfriend's favorite T-shirt to clean the bathroom floor, everything changed. I fell in love.

All of the fun I was having when I was single instantly doubled when I met Keith. We did everything together, from kissing our way through movies to traveling the globe. After all, what could be more fun than falling in *love?*

After we got married, we discovered something new about fun: It was an instant marriage counselor. As I learned from my parents, who have been married for more than forty years, a couple that plays together, stays together. Whenever our marriage would hit the pitfalls that all marriages do, Keith and I would push the pause button and reconnect by having a good time. We'd invite a crew over for a spontaneous paella party and raid our wine cellar. We'd spend a rainy Sunday in bed reading the *New York Times* from cover to cover. Once, we were in the mood to sit at an outdoor café and people-watch, so that's what we did—in Paris.

The proof was in the crème brûlée. Fun, like love, grows exponentially when shared. So after a couple of years we decided to enlarge the party and start a family.

We tried and tried and tried, and after two years of monthly disappointments, we coaxed our child into the world with the help of fertility drugs. Science eventually prevailed, and God answered our prayer with a healthy, happy baby boy. We named him Chase, having no clue that that was exactly how we'd be spending our time.

Then the weirdest thing happened. As soon as I had one, I needed another. *Needed*. As if babies were potato chips! It was like my biological clock suddenly kicked in at the age of forty. I desperately wanted at least a shot at having a girl, and if not, a baby brother for Chase would be fine by me.

My husband, however, was not so sure. Spending the next year in the fertility doctor's office, with me on the chemically induced raging-hormone ride, while we were still getting to know our new family member, was just not something Keith was up for. I more than understood his perspective, and it was decided. We were not going to have another baby. I had a good long cry, said good-bye to my imaginary daughter, and focused on embracing the blessings I had.

Do you believe in miracles? The next morning I woke up and figured I'd use the E.P.T. pregnancy test that had been standing ready, just in case. I was pregnant! No drugs, no doctors, just hockey without the goalie. Four months later, the geneticist informed us that the baby had all the right chromosomes, including the coveted XX combination. Deep sobs erupted from my chest like doves bursting from a too-small cage. I know that I should have been thankful that the baby was healthy, but the truth was, I was *overjoyed*, overwhelmed, over-the-moon, that I was having a girl.

When Mackenzie debuted to the world a pink peony of perfect health, Keith and I could not stop pinching ourselves. That is, until several weeks later, when the dark clouds started rolling in.

Fast-forward one month to the three of us on the beach: Isobel, me, and my recent diagnosis of major depressive disorder. "I just don't get it," I told her. "How could someone so lucky be depressed? I have two healthy kids, yet I can't enjoy them. And I'm *years* away from Nudie Scarf Dancing."

"Things will get better," she assured me. "You're just at the hardest part."

Isobel had a point, and her ideas *were* encouraging. So I sent out an SOS e-mail to my other girlfriends seeking advice, laughs, and suggestions for how to enjoy this roller-coaster ride called motherhood.

The flurry of answers came back fast and furious. First the funny, if dark, one-liners.

"Report yourself (anonymously) to Child Protective Services and have your children taken away for a day or two, instant vacation! Ha, ha!" wrote Krisha Mahoney, Boston, mother of two under two.

"Fly first-class and let your husband and kids fly coach. When you hear howls from the rear of the craft, pretend you don't know them," suggested Meredith Berkman, New York City, mother of three.

"Put a rubber band around your sink sprayer, so when your kids turn on the water, they get squirted in the face, always good for a laugh!" shared Mary Fehrnstrom, San Francisco, mother of three.

Then the practical tips:

"Plan a playdate with other mothers in the park. Bring a cooler filled with wine and juice boxes, and order out for pizza," suggested Karen Hamilton, a mother of three in Rye, New York. "Dinner's all taken care of, and it's fun for you because you are with other moms."

"Steal your kids away for one-on-one dates," e-mailed Laura Quill, a mother of four in San Francisco. "Play cards, or go for nature walks and look for *treasures*. Nothing fancy, just make each child feel special."

Then I got an e-mail that shifted my perspective. It was from Marilyn Terrell, a colleague whom I didn't know well, just enough to know she was still sane after raising five teenagers.

"I remember biking around with my firstborn on a weekday and watching all these serious-looking adults doing important things. And meanwhile I could waste time, lie on the grass, make funny noises, or wear a *ridiculous* hat, and nobody would think I was nuts because I had a kid with me. What a great ploy!" she wrote. "Years later I realized that I could also blame my house being a wreck on the kids. They're a great excuse for having fun, and for not doing housework."

I decided to give it a whirl. I'm not a funny-hat kind of girl, so I grabbed the kids and set out to see the pandas at the zoo. We were in the car on our way, when something magical happened.

From the front seat, I lowered Chase's window. Well. Shock and awe. Chase's golden brown eyes widened at his disappearing window like he had just witnessed a miracle. And maybe he had. His mother's joy was jump-started by his own. Chase's look of pure and utter amazement shifted something inside me.

Soon after, my mother came to visit. Holding Mackenzie, she worked her hands up my daughter's legs, squeezing just so. When she got right above Mackenzie's chubby knees, my then four-month-old laughed for the first time in her life. The sound penetrated me like a Tibetan gong.

"Do it again, Mom," I begged.

Mom did, and Mackenzie laughed again. We did this over and over until I fully understood the pull of addiction.

I started to pay attention, really pay attention, to my kids. I was quickly rewarded with another lesson. I was blowing bubbles with Chase, when he grabbed the little plastic wand. As I watched him struggle to blow one himself, I felt his impatience, and I wished he were old enough for me to explain that this skill would probably take a few more months to master. Then, lo and behold, he blew a bubble! Then another and another. The lesson was clear: What could *I* do that I was impatiently telling myself I couldn't?

It occurred to me that reconnecting with joy wasn't a skill set I had to master, but rather a possibility that I might open myself up to. So I tried my friends' suggestions—not the one about turning myself in to the authorities, but many others that you'll read about in the following pages. Slowly but surely, one good time after another, the depression began to lift. Chase and Mackenzie were my guides as I let go of my expectations and allowed the fun to take whatever form it fancied.

Around this time, I read a magazine article that boiled down happiness into twelve traits: humor, optimism, sense of choice, proactivity, security, spirituality, courage, altruism, love, perspective, purpose, and good health. Strangely, the ideas in this book fit perfectly into these categories. Since, as I've discovered, fun *is* the verb of happiness, maybe this isn't so surprising. If we want enduring satisfaction, the article went on to suggest, we have to maintain a mind-set that allows us to always be on the lookout for small miracles.

Mothers have these small miracles in their lives every day. They are our children. And the time to enjoy them is right now. Turn the page, and let the good times roll.

What's your favorite flavor of fun? Please tell me at www.MelinaBellows.com.

Watch your kids catch fireflies.
Teach them kindness by
letting the insects go.

Children require guidance and sympathy
far more than instruction.

✳ Anne Sullivan

Turn off all the lights and watch a thunderstorm.
Count the seconds between the lightning and the thunder
(explaining that for every second, the storm center is
a mile away). Afterward, go *puddle-jumping*.
Wear old clothes, and tell your kids to get soaking wet.
Have towels warming in the dryer for when they come in.

Throw a theme party when your family least expects it.
For example, Christmas in Mexico.
Serve authentic Mexican cuisine with green and red
margaritas for the grown-ups, and be sure to
have a piñata in the living room (it's always fun to
watch Grandpa dive onto the candy). This will take
your kids' minds off Santa for a second and beats
sitting around drinking eggnog and listening
to the *Christmas with the Chipmunks* album.

Pillage your kids'
Halloween candy
(while they sleep).

$\mathcal{L}$earn the words to show tunes and sing together all over the house and in the car. Do a $\mathit{Chinese\ fire\ drill}$ at the red light in the middle of your town.

It goes without saying that you should never have more children than you have car windows.

* Erma Bombeck

TEN GREAT SOUND TRACKS

Rent

Hairspray

Wicked

The Lion King

Annie

Chicago

Grease

Andrew Lloyd Webber, The Greatest Songs

Fame

Mamma Mia!

Take your kids to as many
major-league-baseball parks
as possible. Save the ticket stubs
and pin them to a large map
to remember all of the
cities and states you've visited.

Pray with your kids every night.

Take time to let them mention all that they
are thankful for, including Mom, Dad,
brothers, sisters, and grandparents.
Encourage each child to share which part
of their day they are most thankful for.

When you're really tired,
hand your little ones a brush,
point to your head, and tell them
to play *beauty parlor*. When you
are really, really tired, tell your
kids that you are playing *princess*
and that you get to be
Sleeping Beauty.

$\mathcal{G}$ive each child a package of sidewalk chalk.
Let them go wild in the driveway, creating hopscotch
templates, elaborate tracks for toy cars, ten-foot-wide pizzas,
and outlines of each other by tracing around their bodies.

(When you come out looking like a pinhead
with really big hips, convince yourself it's just
their inexperience at tracing.)

Take your mother to a spa.
While you are getting seaweed
wraps, tell her all of your
favorite memories of growing up.
Thank her for all that she did for you.

Only a mother knows a mother's fondness.

* *Lady Mary Wortley Montagu*

Make chocolate Mud Slide Cookies together.

Bonus: The measuring helps with math skills,
the pouring helps with coordination, the cleanup helps
with responsibility, and eating the batter helps with PMS.
(Oh, that one's for you.)

• MUD SLIDE COOKIES •

Makes about 50 cookies

4 ounces unsweetened chocolate
12 ounces semisweet chocolate
4 tablespoons (½ stick) butter
4 eggs
1 ⅔ cups sugar
½ teaspoon salt
1 teaspoon vanilla extract
½ cup all-purpose flour
¾ teaspoon baking powder
14 ounces chocolate chips
1 cup chopped walnuts

Preheat the oven to 325° F.

. . . .

Melt the unsweetened and semisweet chocolate and butter in a bowl over gently simmering water.

. . . .

Beat the eggs with the sugar and salt until pale. Gently stir in the melted chocolate, and add the vanilla.

. . . .

Sift the flour and baking powder together. Whisk the flour mixture into the batter, then fold in the chips and nuts.

. . . .

Level scoops of dough in a 1-ounce ice cream scoop, and place a few inches apart on sheet pans lined with parchment paper.

. . . .

Bake for 12 to 15 minutes, or until the tops are just cracked.

. . . .

Do not overbake. The centers should be gooey, hot out of the oven. Add vanilla ice cream at your own peril.

Recipe courtesy of Lindblad Expeditions.

Watch *The Daily Show* with your teenagers.
Talk to them about current events.

Make *bird pudding* to feed to your wild feathered friends.

Mix together 1 cup hot water,
1 cup peanut butter,
2 cups oatmeal,
1 cup flour,
and 4 cups wild bird seed.

Spread the pudding inside a bird feeder.
Get a bird watcher's guide from the library so you can
learn all the names of your flighty friends.

Take a bath with your infant.
Make sure that your husband is
around for the handoff, so you can
relax until the last minute.

(Don't forget to smell your baby
right afterward. Heaven!)

What feeling is so nice as a child's hand in yours?
So small, so soft and warm, like a kitten huddling
in the shelter of your clasp.

✳ Marjorie Holmes

At the end of every summer,
take a family photo for the holiday card
(you'll be happy to have this already accomplished
once December rolls around). Every year, add a framed
11 by 14-inch print to your front hall. Your kids
will be proud now and laugh later at the funny styles.

In the fall, plant bulbs with your kids.
Watch them watch in wonder as the daffodils,
tulips, and hyacinths pop up in the spring.

Get to know your kids one on one.

Steal each away for a date now and then.
Head to Starbucks and let your child
pick out the pastry; then play cards. Or go to the
bookstore and indulge your child in a new book.
The outing doesn't need to be fancy;
the point is to make each child feel special.

On **Saint Patrick's Day**, dye the milk and eggs **green** and turn the furniture upside down, so your home looks like total **chaos**. When your little ones wake up, tell them that the *leprechauns* came. (They won't believe their eyes!)

Is nothing in life ever straight and clear, the way children see it?

※ Rosie Thomas

Flirt with your son's Little League coach.

(But only if he's cute.)

Give yourself a big bonus as the CEO of your family.

Tip: Be generous. A recent study found that you'd have to pay someone $134,121 a year to do all the things a stay-at-home mom does. Moms who work outside the home would still earn $85,876 for their cleaning, driving, and other duties.

The next time you have to go
to a boring *kiddie* activity,
invite another mom-friend along.
Hide chardonnay in two
sippy cups for the two of you
to nurse undercover.

$\mathcal{C}$elebrate a holiday with a family in the neighborhood who practices a different religion.

$\mathcal{P}$lay Freaky Friday with your husband and switch roles for a day. Enjoy his renewed appreciation for his **Super Mom** wife.

Write your kids secret messages in lemon juice
with a paintbrush. (They can read them by
warming them with a heating pad.)

In the dead of winter, make popcorn,
get under warm quilts, and watch
The March of the Penguins on DVD.
Tell your kids you love them even more
than the penguins love their chicks.

Take your kids to a dude ranch.

Invite your friends over with their kids
for a scavenger hunt. Put things on the list
like a 2005 penny, a Chinese-takeout menu, a roll of
toilet paper, something that starts with
the letter F, etc. The adults will walk the street
with a "mobile bar" (a red wagon filled with
cold beers, wine, and juice boxes).

Start a mother-and-daughter book club with your neighbors and their teen daughters.

Suggested Reading List:

To Kill a Mockingbird—Harper Lee
The Princess Diaries—Meg Cabot
Harry Potter Series—J. K. Rowling
Tuck Everlasting—Natalie Babbitt
The Grapes of Wrath—John Steinbeck
Anne of Green Gables— L. M. Montgomery
Pride and Prejudice—Jane Austen
The Sisterhood of the Traveling Pants—Ann Brashares
Watership Down—Richard Adams
The Hobbit—J. R. R. Tolkien
Life of Pi—Yann Martel
The Chronicles of Narnia—C. S. Lewis
The Princess Bride—William Goldman
Hoot—Carl Hiaasen

Run a *lemonade* stand with your children and donate the proceeds to charity.

Take your daughters to get *manicures,*
and be sure to pick a salon with massage chairs.
Let them pick out their own colors and add-on designs.
This will help them get used to the "good life"
so they know the importance of marrying rich.
(Only kidding.)

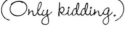

Go to the *beach* in the off-season.

Throw rocks in the water and collect sea glass.
Put the pieces in a vase and use it as a
shelf decor in your living room.

$\mathcal{L}$et your kids make and serve you dinner.
Nothing too complicated, and set out the ingredients
to help them. They must eat, too. Laugh, and follow it up
with a trip to the *ice cream parlor*.

Ask your child what he wants for dinner
only if he's buying.

✳ *Fran Lebowitz*

Go fishing.

Squeamish moms can use raw bacon for bait,
brave ones worms. Tell stories about sea serpents
and the Giant Squid as you wait for a bite.

Participate in a local **fun-run**
and then go out for a *big* breakfast.

Have your kids get dressed up and
play staff at your dinner parties. Employ a doorman,
waitress, butler, and sous-chef.

Get everyone in your family to write down
one fun outing—
such as a trip to a museum, the zoo,
the lake, etc.—and put all the suggestions in a jar.
Every Saturday, one person gets to draw an outing,
and the whole family participates.

Host a
princess tea party
playdate for your girls.
Everyone gets to come
dressed up, the moms, too.
Break out the good china,
and serve tea sandwiches and
your favorite cookies.

After dinner, pull out
the *photo albums* and tell
your teens stories about
what they were like as babies
and toddlers.

On a road trip, listen to Harry Potter on tape
(or for younger families Curious George).
Then tape your own stories.

Skip the Raffi and Barney.
Turn your kids on to **Bob Marley**,
They Might Be Giants, and **Sting**.

If you live in the city with small children,
take them on an urban *safari*. Don pith helmets
and go down to the basement of your apartment building
to look for rats and mice.

Your cri de coeur is "Squeak, squeak."
Bonus points for spotting scuttling water bugs.

Take the baby out to the movies at night.
(They love the dark, and loud trailers
make them snooze immediately.)
Then you can take out the frappuccinos and leftover pizza
you've smuggled in the diaper bag.

Play mad, sad, and glad at the dinner table.
Everyone gets a turn telling what made him or her
feel this way today.

Take a family vacation to **Nantucket**.

(Go with another family and split the cost and double the fun.)

Make sure the home has a big wraparound porch
and puffy hydrangeas and is within walking distance
of the ocean. Each night, build a bonfire on the beach.
Make sure to have lots of marshmallows and sweatshirts.
Take turns telling ghost stories.

Play night Frisbee.

(Use a glow-in-the-dark disc so no one bonks you on the head.)

Buy yourself that Cartier watch, strand of opera-length pearls, or whatever piece of expensive jewelry that you've been lusting after. Justify your purchase by rationalizing that you'll pass it down to your daughter (or your son's wife) eventually.

$\mathcal{M}$ake a family outing of going to a pick-your-own-strawberry farm; learn new recipes for strawberry jam and ice cream.

• MAKE ICE CREAM IN FIVE MINUTES! •

Makes 4 double servings

You will need:
4 gallon-size resealable freezer bags
Ice cubes
2 cups kosher salt
4 quart-size resealable bags
4 cups half-and-half or low-fat milk
$\frac{1}{2}$ cup sugar
2 teaspoons vanilla extract
4 cups chopped strawberries
4 dish towels

Fill each of the gallon-size bags half full with ice. Add 1/2 cup of the kosher salt.

In each quart bag, mix 1 cup of the half-and-half or milk, 2 tablespoons of the sugar, 1/2 teaspoon of the vanilla, and 1 cup of the strawberries. Seal tightly.

Place a small bag inside each large bag. Seal the large bags tightly, so they won't leak.

To protect your hands from the cold, wrap the dish towels around the outside of the large bags. Shake for about 5 minutes, until the half-and-half mixture turns into ice cream.

Use the dish towels to wipe the salt off the outside of the small bags. Then grab spoons and dig in!

Go find mini nature treasures in the woods. Bring some **gorp with M&M's** to nibble as you walk.

Perhaps we have been misguided into taking too much responsibility from our children, leaving them too little room for discovery.

✳ Helen Hayes

Recall Jodie Foster's famous
Oscar acceptance speech,
when she thanked her mother,
"who taught me that all my
finger paints were Picassos
and I didn't have to be afraid."

**Live your life by how you'd
want your children to thank you
from the podium.**

When things get really hairy with the kids,
remind yourself that it's great material
for a story later. Fast-forward and imagine yourself
as a guest on the *Late Show with David Letterman*
when you will regale the audience with your
courageous Domestic Goddess tale.

To the Family—that dear octopus
from whose tentacles we never quite escape nor,
in our inmost hearts, ever quite wish to.

✳ Dodie Smith, *Dear Octopus*

Put a rubber band around your *sink sprayer*, so when your kids turn on the water, they get squirted in the face.

Always good for a laugh.

Teach your kids how to make pancakes.

Train your older ones to do it for the younger ones,
so you and your husband can sleep late on Sundays.

A child of one can be taught not to do certain things,
such as touch a hot stove, turn on the gas,
pull lamps off their tables by their cords,
or wake Mommy before noon.

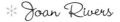
❋ Joan Rivers

Teach your kids eleven ways to say *hello*:
Have them practice on the neighbors.

Japanese: *Konichiwa* (koh-NEE-chee-wah)

Spanish: *Hola* (OH-lah)

Mandarin (Chinese): *Ni hao* (nee haOW)

French: *Bonjour* (bohn-ZHOOR)

Swahili (African): *Jambo* (JAM-bo)

German: *Guten Tag* (GOOT-en tahk)

Arabic: *Al salaam a'alaykum*

(ahl sah-LAHM ah ah-LAY-koom)

Italian: *Buon giorno* (bwohn JOR-noh)

Hindi (India): *Namaste* (nah-mah-STAY)

Russian: *Zdravstvuite* (zzDRAST-vet-yah)

Hebrew (Israel): *Shalom* (sha-LOHM)

Make a *gingerbread house* together.

Take a picture before you let your kids demolish
and devour their architectural digest.

Teach your kids proper etiquette
by having a "*good manners*" meal, where everyone
must eat with proper table manners.
On April Fools' Day,
have a "*bad manners*" meal, where you allow elbows
on the table and eating with mouths open.

Get a dog.

Go for family walks together.

Grow a *sunflower* house in your backyard. Plant seeds in a U shape, and when they grow tall, twine the tops together. Add some *morning glories* for variety. By August, you'll have a happy hut.

In the summer, go to the local crab shack. Sit outside at a newspaper-covered picnic table and order up a bucket of steaming crabs. Smack them open with wooden mallets right on the table. No plates. Just lots of napkins and a bucket. Let your kids do most of the pounding, while you wield the sharper instruments. You'll spend an hour pounding away for scraps of the delicious meat, while getting incredibly messy.

Take your kids to live music performances from very early ages. Inexpensive and outdoors are great to start with in case you might need to make a hasty exit (like when a diaper explodes or your husband starts snoring).

Use your kids as an excuse to do the things you
really want to do, like going to silly feel-good movies,
eating mac and cheese for dinner, and
jumping in the moonbounce.
Use your kids as an excuse to get out of things
you don't want to do, like going to a second
cousin's wedding or your office party.

$\mathcal{L}$et your teenage daughter stay home for an impromptu "snow day." Take her to a fancy department store for a complimentary makeover, and then be *Ladies Who Lunch*. On the way home, tell her that she looks even more beautiful without the makeup, and share with her one of Audrey Hepburn's favorite poems— "Time-Tested Beauty Tips" by Sam Levenson:

For attractive lips, speak words of kindness.
For lovely eyes, seek out the good in people.
For a slim figure, share your food with the hungry.
For beautiful hair, let a child run his fingers through it once
    a day.
For poise, walk with the knowledge you'll never walk alone.
People, even more than things, have to be restored, renewed,
    revived, reclaimed, and redeemed; never throw out anybody.
Remember, if you ever need a helping hand, you'll find one at
    the end of your arm.
As you grow older, you will discover that you have two hands;
    one for helping yourself, the other for helping others.

Every year before the holidays, place a big box in the playroom and invite your kids to fill it with old toys for the needy. Bring them with you to drop it off.

Fly first-class and let your husband and kids fly coach.

When you hear howls from the rear of the craft, pretend you don't know them.

The real menace in dealing with a five-year-old is that in no time at all you begin to sound like a five-year-old.

✳ Jean Kerr

Expose your kids to art.

The bigger and more colorful the paintings, the better. (Rothko, Klee, and Matisse are all winners for beginners.) Then come home and pull out the finger paints, markers, and clay.

Count down to a special occasion like a birthday,
Christmas, Hanukkah, or a visit from the grandparents
by making a paper chain with each ring equal to a day.
Make a ceremony of tearing off a ring each day
and watching the chain get shorter. (It's a great
short-term calendar for pre-readers, to whom
a week can be an eternity.)

$\mathcal{L}$isten for the deep, happy sighs
that come after your kids play or laugh really hard.
Tuck them away in your heart.

Most mothers are instinctive philosophers.

❋ Harriet Beecher Stowe

Host a neighborhood Easter egg hunt.
Make sure the kids hop three times
after they find each egg—

it's fun to watch.

Drive your older kids with their friends
and **just listen**. (For some odd reason,
they think you can't hear when you're driving,
and you'll learn a lot about how they fit in
with their peers and what is important to them.)

Regard your children as Buddhas sent here
to teach you the lessons you need to learn in life.

Lessons kids are Zen masters at:

Living in the moment
Trying everything
Never holding a grudge
Never judging
Being curious about the world

IMPRESS YOUR KIDS WITH
THIS DO-IT-YOURSELF

instant geyser.

(Moms, be careful; this really works!)

1. Position an open bottle of Coke outside on the ground or on a table where it will not tip over.
2. Unwrap a roll of Mentos and position the package over the bottle so that all the candies will drop into the bottle at the same time.
3. Warn all spectators to stand back!
4. Drop the Mentos into the bottle, and move away as fast as you can. *Instant fountain!*

Play *musical* chores.

Blast your favorite song and see
who can clean up their room the most
before the music stops.

On a hot summer day,
make everyone huge
waffle ice cream cones.

Go outside and let them drip
all over the place. Then run
through the sprinkler—in your
clothes—before leading the charge
in a water-balloon fight.

Every Mother's Day, have a picture taken
with your kids. Keep the photos all together—
along with special birthday cards, ticket stubs,
mementos, and anything else that makes you feel good
about being a mom—in an empty Gucci box.

(Of course, you must get those new shoes you love
in order to do this correctly.)

Every year look through your Goddess Mom box and see
how much your kids have grown.

Blame your house being a wreck on your kids.

(Even though you know it would be equally messy
if you had no kids at all.)

Have you and your husband dress up as **dorks**
and visit your teen at school with a *birthday* cake.
(Or if you think this would do more harm than good,
threaten them by staging a dress rehearsal at home.)

Keep pictures of your kids at very young ages
in your office or your brag book,
so strangers will assume that you are younger.

Make your kids a special
breakfast on **Valentine's Day**:
waffles with strawberries
and whipped cream, red candles,
and cards telling each one
how much you love them.

Making the decision to have a child is momentous.
It is to decide forever to have your heart
go walking around outside your body.

✳ Elizabeth Stone

On a *blustery* day, put on raincoats and scoot to the library. Come home and have reading hour in your living room. Before you settle in, teach your kids to make their own cocoa by stirring two tablespoons of chocolate chips into a mug of hot milk.

Two words:

Family Karaoke.

Videotape your kids lip-synching, so you have
some leverage for when they start dating.

Invent a house fairy.

Give her a name, and tell your kids
that she is always watching them and counting up
their good deeds.

To get your teens to talk,
play *two truths* and a lie.
Tell your children three things
about your day, two real and
one made up. Your children
guess which is the lie.
Then it's their turn.

There is nothing more thrilling in this world,
I think, than having a child that is yours,
and yet is mysteriously a stranger.

* *Agatha Christie*

On a crisp fall Saturday,
invite everyone you know
to a child-parent
touch football game
à la the Kennedy clan.

Have a

watermelon-seed-spitting contest

with your kids in the backyard.

Pick a special anniversary
and renew your vows with your husband.
Let your kids participate in the ceremony.
(Better yet, leave them home with Grandma,
and do it on the Spanish Steps in Rome.)

Teach your kids to play
poker.

$\mathcal{L}$earn all of the *emoticons* behind your kids' backs, and surprise them with text messages.

:-)	Smile
:-[	Embarrassed
O:-)	Innocent
:-\	Undecided
:'(	Crying
:-X	Lips-are-sealed
:-D	Laughing
:-(	Frowning
;-)	Winking
:-P	Sticking-out-tongue
=-O	Surprised
:-*	Kissing

Plan a late-afternoon playdate with other moms at the playground or beach. Pack up coolers with *juice boxes* and *vino*, and have *pizzas* delivered. Feeding kids dinner becomes fun, because you're doing it with other moms.

Let your whole family take a "*day off*" and hang out in pj's all day long.

Ride a
roller coaster
with your kids.
Front row, in the dark.

Show no fear.

Star in your own version of the movie *Home Alone.* Send your kids out with your husband for an afternoon of errands. Savor some quiet time in the house. (Resist the urge to clean it.)

When you are a mother, you are never really alone in your thoughts. You are connected to your child and to all those who touch your lives. A mother always has to think twice, once for herself and once for her child.

✳ *Sophia Loren*

Take your kids to a yoga class (or drumming circle). Make sure to get there early, so you can *gossip* with the other moms.

Then cleanse yourself with the *asanas*.

A recent study asked kids the question

"If kids ruled the world, what would you change?"

The answer:

"We'd have two Halloweens!"

Host a Halloween party the night before.
Invite all of your neighbors to come and carve pumpkins.
Put candles in all of the jack-o'-lanterns and line the
pumpkins up on the deck while the kids dunk for apples
and the adults enjoy Oktoberfest beer. Serve chili.
Have a costume competition where everyone gets a prize.

• HALLOWEEN CHILI •

Makes 6 servings

1 pound lean ground turkey

1 large onion, chopped (about 1 cup)

2 garlic cloves, crushed

1 tablespoon chili powder

$\frac{1}{2}$ teaspoon salt

1 teaspoon ground cumin

1 teaspoon dried oregano

1 teaspoon unsweetened cocoa

$\frac{1}{2}$ teaspoon red pepper sauce, or to taste

One 16-ounce can whole tomatoes, undrained

One 15- or 16-ounce can red kidney beans, undrained

Cook the turkey, onion, and garlic in a 3-quart saucepan over medium-high heat for about 8 minutes, stirring occasionally, until the turkey is brown; drain.

. . . .

Stir in all of the remaining ingredients except the beans, breaking up the tomatoes. Heat to boiling; reduce the heat to low. Cover and simmer for 1 hour, stirring occasionally.

. . . .

Stir in the beans. Heat to boiling; reduce the heat to low. Simmer uncovered for about 20 minutes, stirring occasionally, until the chili reaches the desired thickness.

. . . .

Serve with bowls of chopped tomatoes, chopped onions, shredded lettuce, shredded cheese, sour cream, and broken corn chips to sprinkle on top.

Pitch a tent in the backyard.

Use it as your outdoor reading room. Or when
it's a full moon, plan a family campout with tents,
sleeping bags, a transistor radio, and s'mores, of course.

Shortcut recipe:

put roasted marshmallows between
LU Petite Écolier biscuits.

Take your teenage son
with you to test-drive the Maserati,
Ferrari, or Porsche convertible
of your *dreams.*

Take your daughter shoe shopping.
In Paris.

Whenever your kids are
about to eat something delicious,
inform them you are "quality testing"
and take the first bite.

Give your kids "quiet time" every day.
Let them learn to be by themselves with books,
crayons, or LEGO blocks.

A mother is not a person to lean on
but a person to make leaning unnecessary.

* Dorothy Canfield Fisher

Grow peas and beans in the summer.
Let the kids pick, wash, and prepare them
each night for supper.

Demonstrate the latest steps
you learned in your
Latin dance class
for your teenage daughters
and their friends.

Watch them laugh their heads off.

Rent *Sex and the City* on DVD.

As you watch, reminisce about the good old days
when you were single and the biggest problem you had
was if the "He" of the moment was going to call.
Let the romance of your carefree youth seduce you.
Then remember that along with that freedom
came a crushing anxiety—all you really wanted
was to fall in love and give birth to beautiful babies.

In the movie *It's a Wonderful Life,*
every time a bell rings, an angel gets his wings.

Every time you hear your children belly-laugh,
remind yourself that you've earned yours.

Watch your kids as they sleep.
Feel your heart *overflow* with love.